SEXUAL HARASSMENT IN THE WORKPLACE

A Guide to Prevention

Juliana Lightle, Ph.D.
and Elizabeth H. Doucet, Esq.

CRISP PUBLICATIONS, INC.
Los Altos, California

SEXUAL HARASSMENT IN THE WORKPLACE
A Guide to Prevention

**Juliana Lightle, Ph.D.
and Elizabeth H. Doucet, Esq.**

CREDITS:
Editor: **Bev Manber**
Designer: **Carol Harris**
Typesetting: **ExecuStaff**
Cover Design: **Carol Harris**
Artwork: **Ralph Mapson**

Copyright © 1992 Crisp Publications, Inc.
Printed in the United States of America by Bawden Printing Company.

English language Crisp books are distributed worldwide. Our major international distributors include:

CANADA: Reid Publishing, Ltd., Box 69559—109 Thomas St., Oakville, Ontario Canada L6J 7R4. TEL: (416) 842-4428; FAX: (416) 842-9327

AUSTRALIA: Career Builders, P.O. Box 1051, Springwood, Brisbane, Queensland, Australia 4127. TEL: 841-1061, FAX: 841-1580

NEW ZEALAND: Career Builders, P.O. Box 571, Manurewa, Auckland, New Zealand. TEL: 266-5276, FAX: 266-4152

JAPAN: Phoenix Associates Co., Mizuho Bldg. 2-12-2, Kami Osaki, Shinagawa-Ku, Tokyo 141, Japan. TEL: 3-443-7231, FAX: 3-443-7640

Selected Crisp titles are also available in other languages. Contact International Rights Manager Tim Polk at (415) 949-4888 for more information.

Library of Congress Catalog Card Number 91-78106
Lightle, Juliana and Doucet, Elizabeth H.
Sexual Harassment in the Workplace
ISBN 1-56052-153-8

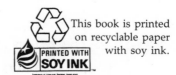

This book is printed on recyclable paper with soy ink.

AUTHORS' NOTES

We all want a safe, secure, enjoyable place to work. We want to produce good work and contribute to our workplace.

Unfortunately, for substantial numbers of men and women, sexual harassment interferes. It not only affects them negatively as individuals, but also negatively affects their colleagues, their department—indeed, the entire organization. People who feel harassed cannot focus on their work, have increased absenteeism, experience high anxiety, and sometimes experience illness due to the stress. This obviously impacts everyone around them.

Sexual harassment can be eliminated. We can have positive, fun and productive workplaces. We can set a tone in our organizations that creates trust, security, achievement and excellence.

This book looks at sexual harassment from two vantage points.

- Prevention—how to create a positive workplace
- The legal aspects—what to do when someone files a complaint

This book will help you look at your own attitudes and feelings about others in the workplace, about differences and how you deal with them. We cannot create positive workplaces until we all understand our own and others' dynamics, and what causes negative and inappropriate behaviors. We need to learn new effective behaviors, and to establish a positive climate.

We invite you to a new vision of the workplace, free of harassment and ineffectual, divisive behaviors, an open workplace in which people can joke and have fun and be productive without hurting others.

You will find this book most useful if you complete the exercises. If you are not in a management or human resources position within your organization, we invite you to share this book with your management and human resources staff. Working together, you can create a positive, secure, productive, fun-filled work environment.

Elizabeth H. Doucet

Juliana Lightle

i

CONTENTS

SOME IMPORTANT OBJECTIVES FOR THE READER

Sexual harassment in the workplace is of great concern to employers and employees. We hope this book will offer some insight into the issues related to sexual harassment. As you read this book, think about what you hope to *accomplish*.

Check the objectives below that are important to you. When you complete this book, review your objectives and feel the sense of achievement from what you have learned.

After Reading This Book You Will Be Able To:

☐ 1. Understand the concept of sexual harassment.

☐ 2. Recognize those actions that would be considered sexual harassment, in violation of federal, state and local laws.

☐ 3. Take steps to modify behavior that could be viewed as sexual harassment.

☐ 4. Set up procedures within your organization to handle claims of sexual harassment, including developing a policy and implementing training for employees and supervisors.

☐ 5. Effectively work with administrative agencies investigating claims of sexual harassment.

☐ 6. Contribute to an exciting, positive workplace that is free of sexual harassment.

☐ 7. Make decisions affecting employees who are the victims of sexual harassment.

TEST YOUR KNOWLEDGE →

TEST YOUR KNOWLEDGE OF SEXUAL HARASSMENT

Before beginning this book, check your current knowledge of sexual harassment. Take a few minutes and respond to the questions below, circling true or false where appropriate.

		True	False
1.	Sexual harassment only concerns women who work.	T	F
2.	An organization that has a policy that prohibits sexual harassment in the workplace will be insulated from charges and lawsuits alleging sexual harassment.	T	F
3.	The only way an organization and its managers can ensure that there are no sexual harassment complaints is to limit relationships among their employees.	T	F
4.	The courts have ruled that in investigating claims of sexual harassment the standard to be applied is that of the reasonable woman.	T	F
5.	Most instances of sexual harassment involve requests for sexual favors.	T	F
6.	Sexual harassment policies must include all employees, even those who are puritanical or prudish.	T	F
7.	If found guilty of sexual harassment, an employee may be individually liable to the harassed employee and may be ordered by the court to pay out-of-pocket expenses not reimbursable by the employer.	T	F

	True	False

8. Under the concept of ''ugly discrimination,'' employees can bring complaints or file lawsuits where employment decisions are based on an employee submitting to sexual harassment and an ''ugly'' employee not being offered the opportunity to submit to such harassment.   T   F

9. Most charges or complaints of sexual harassment are made by troublemakers, since harassment is not a problem in all workplaces.   T   F

10. Sexual harassment is going to occur, regardless of what employers or their employees do to avoid it.   T   F

Correct responses to these questions are on page 111 in the Answers and Solutions section. Do not look now. Wait until you have completed the book, then test your knowledge again.

P A R T

I

What Is
Sexual Harassment?

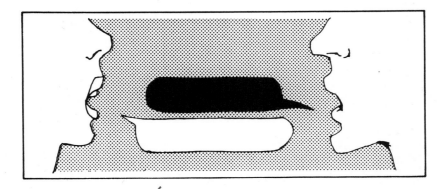

SEXUAL HARASSMENT: A DEFINITION

Although the Civil Rights act of 1964 (Title VII) guaranteed certain rights for all people, the concept of sexual harassment as a legal claim is relatively new.

The concept was first addressed in 1980 by the courts and the Equal Employment Opportunity Commission (EEOC), the United States federal agency that is responsible for enforcing anti-discrimination laws. In 1980, the EEOC issued what are called *Guidelines on Sexual Harassment in the Workplace.* Although guidelines are not law, the United States Supreme Court has said the EEOC *Guidelines* should be accorded the same weight as laws.

These guidelines describe sexual harassment as: ''unwelcome sexual advances, requests for sexual favors and other verbal or physical conduct of a sexual nature. When:

a) Submission to such conduct is made explicitly or implicitly a term or condition of an individual's employment.

b) Submission to or rejection of such conduct by an individual is used as the basis for employment decisions affecting the individual; or,

c) Such conduct has the purpose or effect of unreasonably interfering with an individual's work performance or creating an intimidating, hostile or offensive working environment.''

What actions do *you* believe constitute sexual harassment? As we will discuss later, anyone in the workplace can be sexually harassed. Similarly, anyone in the workplace and even persons not employed by the organization can be accused of and be liable for acts of sexual harassment.

On the next page you will have a chance to test your knowledge and biases.

True or False: What Actions Do You Believe Constitute Sexual Harassment?

Circle true (T) or false (F) for the following questions. Then look on page 113 to see how your answers compare to those of the authors. You may find that it is difficult to respond to some of these situations. Sexual harassment is not easy to define; like all illegal acts of discrimination, it is not always clear and is often a very personal matter, as viewed by the individual affected.

		True	False
1.	Only physical acts by one employee against another constitute sexual harassment.	T	F
2.	A cartoon hanging over an employee's desk constitutes sexual harassment.	T	F
3.	Ignoring another employee constitutes sexual harassment.	T	F
4.	Actions of a sexual nature by nonemployees are sexual harassment.	T	F
5.	Staring at an employee by another is not sexual harassment.	T	F
6.	Dirty jokes or jokes with sexual innuendoes are not sexual harassment.	T	F
7.	Unpermitted touching of one employee by another could never be considered sexual harassment.	T	F
8.	The promotion of a willing participant in an office romance is not sexual harassment.	T	F
9.	Failure to promote an employee because he/she will not date you is sexual harassment.	T	F
10.	Inviting a subordinate to go out on a date even though he/she has refused to go out with you in the past is sexual harassment.	T	F

YOUR DEFINITION

How would you define sexual harassment? Would your definition be different if you were of the opposite gender? Would you define sexual harassment differently if you were a parent? Write your definition below.

_____

_____

_____

_____

_____

_____

_____

Note: Not all agencies or courts define sexual harassment in the same way.

WHAT THE EQUAL EMPLOYMENT OPPORTUNITY COMMISSION SAYS ABOUT SEXUAL HARASSMENT

Sexual harassment has been part of the workplace for many years, accepted as part of the atmosphere or terms and conditions of employment.

In its guidelines, the EEOC stated that the best way for an employer to deal with sexual harassment is to take all necessary steps to prevent it, including ''affirmatively raising the subject, expressing strong disapproval, developing appropriate sanctions, informing employees of their rights to raise the issue, and developing methods to make sure all employees are sensitive to the issue.''

WHAT THE COURTS HAVE SAID ABOUT SEXUAL HARASSMENT

Since the EEOC issued its guidelines, more and more courts, from the lowest to the highest, have struggled with issues related to sexual harassment. Since the late 1980's the courts in the United States have taken an aggressive role in trying to eliminate sexual harassment in the workplace.

Step by step, the courts have dealt with all the issues addressed in the EEOC guidelines. Perhaps the most important decision so far was a Supreme Court case that recognized the concept of sexual harassment and that a hostile work environment could constitute sexual harassment. Other courts have found the existence of sexual harassment in the following situations.

► A male supervisor's demand that a female subordinate submit to his sexual advances was *a condition of employment* within the meaning of the civil rights laws when he told her that her continued success and advancement at the organization were dependent on her agreeing to his sexual demands.

► An employer violated Title VII when one of its male supervisors terminated a female employee in retaliation for her refusing to *submit* to his sexual advances.

► An employee was sexually harassed in violation of Title VII when she was forced to *work in an atmosphere* replete with intimidation and offensive comments of a sexual nature.

► An employee was sexually harassed with regard to the *terms and conditions of her employment* when her supervisors sexually harassed her without her department director intervening. The Court said the employee was not required to show that she resisted the harassment and that she lost or was denied tangible job benefits.

► Homosexual advances by a supervisor toward a male employee is prohibited by Title VII and is sexual harassment.

WHERE DOES SEXUAL HARASSMENT OCCUR?

Sexual harassment takes many forms. For purposes of this workbook we are talking about sexual harassment in the workplace only.

There is no work environment that is totally free from sexual harassment. Circle whether you agree or disagree that sexual harassment occurs in these workplaces, with which we are all familiar.

	Agree	Disagree
• Educational institutions, schools, universities	☐	☐
• Law offices	☐	☐
• Corporate offices	☐	☐
• Banking institutions	☐	☐
• Night clubs or other places of entertainment	☐	☐
• Governmental offices	☐	☐
• Religious institutions	☐	☐

HOW DOES SEXUAL HARASSMENT AFFECT YOUR WORKPLACE?

In 1981, *Redbook Magazine* interviewed 140,000 men and women concerning sexual harassment. Their findings revealed that 80% of the persons interviewed believed they had been sexually harassed. Which type of harassment do you believe was cited most frequently?

_____

_____

The type of harassment most frequently mentioned by those interviewed was that type which created a hostile or offensive work environment; e.g., words, jokes, gestures.

Sexual harassment is damaging to the workplace. It affects the individuals harassed and the person(s) accused, who may be innocent. It can go even further than that. It can generate costly lawsuits, unfavorable publicity or the invasion of privacy. It can affect the bottom line of the employer, be it a school, corporation or governmental entity, as well as reaching into the pocketbook of supervisors, managers and co-workers. Sexual harassment can affect the entire life of an organization and its members.

HOW DOES SEXUAL HARASSMENT AFFECT YOUR WORKPLACE? (continued)

List below the effects you believe sexual harassment has on:

The Victim: _____

_____

_____

_____

The Accused: _____

_____

_____

_____

The Organization: _____

_____

_____

_____

If a person is found to have sexually harassed another individual, the courts may not permit the harasser's employer to pay the court costs, attorney's fees or damages assessed against them! *In a number of cases, the courts have ordered individuals who have been found guilty of harassment to pay these costs themselves.*

In one case, an employee who had been sexually harassed by her supervisor was awarded $50,000 for emotional distress. Another employee was awarded $975,000 in punitive damages when a jury found that the president of the company had forced the employee to have sex with him.

IS SEXUAL HARASSMENT A FORM OF SEX DISCRIMINATION?

Title VII of the Civil Rights Act of 1964 prohibits discrimination in employment. Many people confuse sexual harassment and sex discrimination. In fact, sexual harassment is only one kind of sex discrimination. Both are actions prohibited by state and federal law. (For a further discussion of discrimination on the basis of sex, see *Guide to Affirmative Action* by Conrad and Maddux, listed in the back of this book.)

What actions would be considered discrimination on the basis of sex, but not sexual harassment? List three you believe fall into this category:

1. _____

2. _____

3. _____

In cases of sexual harassment, sex is made a term or condition of employment. In instances of discrimination on the basis of sex, a member or members of one sex are treated differently from those of the other sex. Can an employer who harasses female and male employees similarly be found to have committed sexual harassment? This important question is addressed in Part II.

P A R T

II

EEOC Guidelines and Sexual Harassment

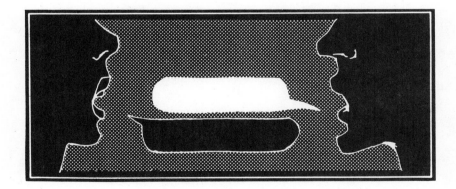

THE EEOC GUIDELINES ON SEXUAL HARASSMENT

Sec. 1604.11 Sexual Harassment

(a) Harassment on the basis of sex is a violation of Sec. 703 of Title VII. Unwelcome sexual advances, requests for sexual favors, and other verbal or physical conduct of a sexual nature constitute sexual harassment when (1) submission to such conduct is made either explicitly or implicitly a term or condition of an individual's employment, (2) submission to or rejection of such conduct by an individual is used as the basis for employment decisions affecting such individual, or (3) such conduct has the purpose or effect of unreasonably interfering with an individual's work performance or creating an intimidating, hostile, or offensive working environment.

(b) In determining whether alleged conduct constitutes sexual harassment, the Commission will look at the record as a whole and the totality of the circumstances, such as the nature of the sexual advances and the context in which the alleged incidents occurred. The determination of the legality of a particular action will be made from the facts, on a case by case basis.

(c) Applying general Title VII principles, an employer, employment agency, joint apprenticeship committee or labor organization (hereinafter collectively referred to as ''employer'') is responsible for its acts and those of its agents and supervisory employees with respect to sexual harassment regardless of whether the specific acts complained of were authorized or even forbidden by the employer and regardless of whether the employer knew or should have known of their occurrence. The Commission will examine the circumstances of the particular employment relationship and the job functions performed by the individual in determining whether an individual acts in either a supervisory or agency capacity.

(d) With respect to conduct between fellow employees, an employer is responsible for acts of sexual harassment in the workplace where the employer (or its agents or supervisory employees) knows or should have known of the conduct, unless it can show that it took immediate and appropriate corrective action.

THE EEOC GUIDELINES ON SEXUAL HARASSMENT (continued)

(e) An employer may also be responsible for the acts of non-employees, with respect to sexual harassment of employees in the workplace, where the employer (or its agents or supervisory employees) knows or should have known of the conduct and fails to take immediate and appropriate corrective action. In reviewing these cases the Commission will consider the extent of the employer's control and any other legal responsibility which the employer may have with respect to the conduct of such non-employees.

(f) Prevention is the best tool for the elimination of sexual harassment. An employer should take all steps necessary to prevent sexual harassment from occurring, such as affirmatively raising the subject, expressing strong disapproval, developing appropriate sanctions, informing employees of their right to raise and how to raise the issue of harassment under Title VII, and developing methods to sensitize all concerned.

(g) Other related practices: Where employment opportunities or benefits are granted because of an individual's submission to the employer's requests for sexual favors, the employer may be held liable for unlawful sex discrimination against other persons who were qualified for but denied that employment opportunity or benefit.

WHO IS THE ACCUSED?

There is no special modus operandi, race, sex or age for accused sexual harassers. They come from all walks of life, all ages, both sexes.

The classic cases are managers or supervisors using their formal power to harass: *if you do not comply, I will fire, not select, whatever the situation allows.* This is referred to as the *quid pro quo* situation. However, harassment also occurs among co-workers and clients, and customers have been known to harass employees.

> **Note:** The organization is usually liable legally when a co-worker harasses, when a client or customer harasses, or when a supervisor or manager harasses and the organization knew, or should have known, about the harassment and took no steps to stop it.

WHO IS LIABLE FOR COSTS AND DEFENDING THE ACTION?

The organization is best served by creating an atmosphere in which individuals feel comfortable addressing the complaint to the appropriate internal staff.

If the individual who has been sexually harassed does seek outside legal counsel, of course, he or she will have to pay that counsel unless the case is taken on a contingency basis. In such cases, the legal counsel obviously has a huge stake in proving the case against the organization.

The organization, the defendant, obviously has to pay for its own legal counsel. But it may have to pay much more if the person raising the claim wins and the court requires the defendant to pay the legal fees and court costs of the injured party. Courts have refused to permit some organizations to pay these costs, ordering the convicted individuals to pay out of their own pockets. The court may award additional damages for emotional distress, etc., in which case the amounts can be huge. Under recent cases, the courts have awarded punitive damages. A 1991 amendment to the federal civil rights laws allows courts to award compensatory and punitive damages in discrimination cases where there are no additional claims, as in claims for breach of contract, emotional distress or other personal injury claims. Awards made possible by this amendment can be substantially higher than losses in a typical sex discrimination case—as high as $300,000 for punitive damages alone—against an organization with 500 or more employees. The price tag for a finding of discrimination against an organization with fewer than 100 employees may go as high as $50,000.

WHO ARE THE VICTIMS?

Nearly all females have at one time or another experienced offensive jokes, catcalls and whistles when on the street. These behaviors often occur outside the workplace and are not related to work in any way. Women learn to deal with these forms of harassment as they grow up, usually by simply ignoring them. But what about harassment at work or school?

A variety of surveys have attempted to measure the extent of harassment in the workplace, from government to corporate environments. In all studies, no fewer than 40 percent of women reported harassment and as many as 45 percent of men, when admiring sexual comments are included as harassment.

In a government study of sexual harassment within the federal government in the early eighties, findings showed that lost time and productivity due to sexual harassment cost the government $188.7 million over a two year period. Forty-two percent of the women and 14 percent of the men stated that they had experienced harassment. When the study was repeated five years later and costs had increased to $267 million, those percentages had not decreased.

In 1991, at two Minnesota high schools, two girls sued their high school when they failed to respond to harassment complaints. Although both were cases of student-to-student harassment, female college students also report high percentages of harassment from male professors. Harassed college students rarely report this abuse because they fear professors will retaliate by giving them poor grades and substandard job recommendations.

FACTS AND FIGURES

WHO ARE THE VICTIMS? (continued)

In their *Guide to Affirmative Action,* Conrad and Maddux cite an Illinois Task Force study:

- Ninety percent of all women surveyed think sexual harassment is a problem

- Seventy percent of all working women surveyed feel they have been harassed at one time or another.

Of those who felt they had been harassed:

- Fifty-two percent had been subjected to sexual remarks or teasing

- Forty-one percent had been the target of suggestive looks or leers

- Twenty-six percent had experienced subtle hints or pressure

- Twenty-five percent had been physically touched against their will or grabbed

- Twenty percent had been propositioned

- Fourteen percent had been repeatedly pressured to engage in a personal relationship

- Nine percent reported other miscellaneous forms of unwanted sexual attention

- Two percent experienced forms of coercive rape.

Although the victim of sexual harassment and the person accused of sexual harassment may be peers, more frequently the victim is in a position of lesser power than the accused. The most common example is the boss-subordinate situation. Harassment also occurs between customers/clients and providers.

WHAT IS THE ACTION?

The different forms of sexual harassment lie on a sexual exploitation continuum:

Increasing physical violence

verbal and visual harassment	physical harassment	rape	rape/ murder

Typical Forms of Harassment

Verbal/Visual

- Risque jokes
- Off-color remarks
- Leers
- Unwanted propositions
- Threats
- Passes
- Suggestive, violent or sexual photographs
- Pin-ups, cartoons
- Unwanted sexual compliments
- Repeated requests for dates
- Repeated requests for sexual favors
- Excessive flirting
- Wearing revealing attire
- Staring

Physical

- Unwanted touching on any part of the body
- Touching of breast and hips
- Unwanted brushing against another's body
- Standing too close
- Excessively ''lengthy'' handshakes
- Physical attack

Harassment may take the form of a risque joke or a more aggressive form, such as repeated inappropriate touching of another body. Whether intentional or not, all sexual harassment is aggression against another person's body or psyche, using sex as the weapon.

YOUR EXPERIENCE

Almost everyone has either experienced harassment personally or knows someone who has. If you have not experienced harassment and do not believe it is prevalent, ask colleagues or friends about their experience. Use the space below to describe a personal experience, either yours or someone else's. Include where it occurred and what form the harassment took.

_____

_____

_____

_____

_____

_____

_____

_____

_____

What about the situation caused you to see it as harassment? How did you feel? *Note:* If you are using a friend's or colleague's experience, do you view it differently than they did? How? Why?

_____

_____

_____

_____

_____

_____

_____

P A R T

III

Preventing Sexual Harassment in the Workplace

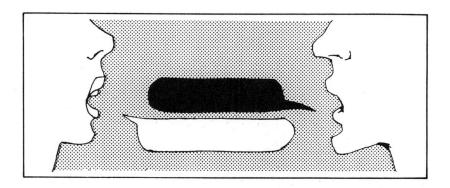

WHY SEXUAL HARASSMENT OCCURS

Judging from historical accounts, sexual harassment has always occured but there was no label for such behavior. The industrial revolution brought about changes in the traditional roles of men and women which greatly increased gender specialization and created a new kind of workplace in the western world. Men and women no longer worked together on the farm or in the family trade. The role of each became more specialized.

This job specialization continued to increase. And as people continued to move to the cities, the need for economic security also increased. People were no longer self-sufficient. Thus, the roles for males and females became increasingly narrow and well-defined, and for the vast majority of people, very comfortable. Everyone knew exactly what was expected and how to behave. There was little, if any, ambiguity. The stereotypical roles of men and women became more extreme. Women became the ''weaker sex'' among the middle and upper classes. Men were expected to be strong and work to support the women and children. Thus, women became increasingly dependent. This gave men much greater power.

In the past few decades things have changed. More and more women have joined the workforce. Increasingly they have moved into jobs that were traditionally held by males. As a result of this change, the balance is shifting. Sexual harassment is one result of this shift. When harassment is committed by a male against a female, it may be a response to real or imagined loss of power. When committed by a woman against a man, it may be an expression of retaliation or a ''flexing'' of the ''new'' power.

GENDER STEREOTYPES

Below is a list of words often used to describe individuals. Beside each word, put an **F** if it is stereotypically female and an **M** if it describes the male stereotype:

_____ Dependent		_____ Cautious
_____ Doer		_____ Kind
_____ Assertive		_____ Leader
_____ Cooperative		_____ Powerful
_____ Competent		_____ Brave
_____ Important		_____ Stoical
_____ Fearful		_____ Unemotional
_____ Risk taker		_____ Decisive
_____ Nice		_____ Warm
_____ Weak		_____ Flexible
_____ Follower		_____ Emotional
_____ Gentle		_____ Aggressive
_____ Competitive		_____ Consistent
_____ Wishy-washy		_____ Protective
_____ Strong		_____ Achiever
_____ Passive		_____ Subjective
_____ Objective		_____ Cheerful
_____ Excitable		_____ Soft Spoken
_____ Moody		_____ Unreliable

The truth is everyone is familiar with these stereotypes. Even if they no longer apply in most situations, stereotypes continue to affect behavior, the way we describe each other and our ways of interrelating.

Now go back over the list. Put a check mark beside every word that applies to you. Most likely you will find you have some combination of both male and female stereotypes. How do you feel when someone attributes the stereotype for your gender to you?

_____

_____

_____

_____

_____

_____

_____

Everyone has stereotypes. The problem with them is how individuals apply them to make inaccurate and unfair comparisons, to prejudge.*

_____

*For an excellent discussion on stereotypes and their effects, see *Men and Women, Partners at Work* by Simons and Weissman, another Crisp Fifty-Minute Series book.

MORE ON WHY SEXUAL HARASSMENT OCCURS

Traditionally, the working world was made up predominantly of men. Women who worked usually did so at specific kinds of jobs, with mostly other women. They held ''appropriate'' jobs, in keeping with the stereotypes. This has changed dramatically in the past several decades. Why has the adjustment been so difficult?

> **CHANGE IS DIFFICULT**
>
> **THE OLD BOXES ARE FALLING APART**
>
> **THERE IS A NEW STRUGGLE FOR POWER AND POSITION**

Men who felt secure with the old way never expected to compete with women. This difficult situation is compounded because there are no new generally accepted, pervasive rules of behavior:

- Should men hold doors open for women?

- Who pays the check when men and women at work have lunch together?

- Who lifts heavy boxes that need to be moved to the department storeroom?

- Can the good old jokes men used to tell each other at meetings be told in front of women?

In the face of these changes, individuals have two choices.

- Adapt

- Struggle more intensively

Sexual harassment is one form of this struggle. Harassment also occurs because organizations and managers allow it to occur. In some cases, they even set a tone that encourages it.

Whatever the reason, sexual harassment is inexcusable. Both men and women harass. Some people cannot adapt. Some will use any means to compete, rather than pursue personal and professional growth. Growth—change—is tedious and exhausting.

DEALING WITH CHANGE

How do *you* deal with change? Write your answer in the space below:

_____

_____

_____

_____

_____

_____

_____

_____

_____

Now describe how you deal with others at work, with men and with women. Ask yourself these questions: Do you respect individuality? Do you expect to be treated first as an individual and second as a woman or man or vice versa? Are you supportive of others, regardless of their gender? Have you ever made a business decision based on the gender of an individual, how you felt about them sexually, or their sexual orientation?

_____

_____

_____

_____

_____

_____

_____

_____

DEALING WITH CHANGE (continued)

Have you ever deliberately flirted at work? If so, what were the circumstances and why did you do it?

_____

_____

_____

_____

_____

_____

Do you wear clothes, cologne, perfume or make-up to enhance, exploit or subdue your gender?

_____

_____

_____

_____

_____

_____

If this is the first time you have thought about these questions, what is your response to them? Surprise, discomfort, what?

_____

_____

_____

_____

_____

_____

A SELF-CHECK FOR MANAGERS

Describe how the men and women who work for you interrelate.

_____

_____

_____

How do you feel about the way the men and women in your area work together?

_____

_____

_____

Which of their behaviors, if any, could be interpreted as sexual harassment? How do you know?

_____

_____

_____

What have you done about it?

_____

_____

_____

How would you feel and what would you do if sexual harassment happened to you?

_____

_____

_____

What kind of tone do you set for your department about sexual harassment?

_____

_____

_____

PREVENTING SEXUAL HARASSMENT IN THE WORKPLACE

When it comes to sexual harassment, to use the old saying, *an ounce of prevention is worth a pound of cure.*

Sexual harassment is very expensive. At the very least, it causes low morale and consequently decreases productivity. Angry, fearful, humiliated people are incapable of performing well. If not addressed, sexual harassment may result in expensive lawsuits, terrible publicity and destruction of an organizational image that took years to build.

Although sexual harassment is illegal, its elimination will come through organizational and individual commitment, not the courts. Most individuals, men and women, want a safe and secure workplace, free from intimidation and fear.

An organization can take an important step toward creating a safe, secure, positive work environment by implementing a strong sexual harassment policy. There are several choices for policy development.

► A broad antiharassment/positive environment policy that includes a statement that specifically addresses sexual harassment

► A separate sexual harassment policy that covers all organizational members

► Separate sexual harassment policies, one that addresses nonmanagement employees and one that addresses management.

Following are four sample policies.

SAMPLE POLICIES AHEAD

Sexual Harassment: Policy 1

To: All Employees

Subject: Working Atmosphere Statement
Policy Against Harassment of Employees

All employees have a responsibility to maintain high standards of honesty and integrity and to conduct themselves in a manner that will assure proper performance of the organization's business.

Working Atmosphere

It is the policy of this organization to provide a working atmosphere free from discriminatory insult, intimidation and other forms of harassment. Furthermore, all employees share the responsibility for fostering a pleasant working atmosphere, which allows individuals to achieve high performance in their duties. Harassment is also prohibited by state and federal antidiscrimination laws.

Harassment

Harassment based on race, religion, color, national origin, age, sexual orientation or sex is a violation of the organization's policy. Harassment may be overt or subtle, but whatever form it takes, verbal, nonverbal or physical, harassment is insulting and demeaning to the recipient and cannot be tolerated in the workplace. Examples of harassment are verbal abuse; racial, ethnic and religious epithets; slurs or jokes; graffiti (remarks written or drawn on walls or other structures); obscene gestures and hazing. Even derogatory remarks between friends may lead to overt acts of discrimination.

Sexual Harassment

Sexual harassment is intolerable in the workplace. It includes unwelcome sexual advances, requests for sexual favors and other verbal or physical conduct of a sexual nature, when such conduct is made explicitly or implicitly a term or condition of employment, is used as a basis for employment decisions, or has the purpose or effect of interfering with work performance or creating an otherwise offensive working environment.

POLICY 1 (continued)

Employee Responsibility

An employee who believes that he/she or some other employee is being harassed by someone on the premises should promptly report the harassing conduct to management. Incidents may be reported to the immediate supervisor, EEO Coordinator, Human Resources Manager or plant management.

Management Responsibility

All members of management are responsible for ensuring that no harassment occurs within their area of authority. Complaints of harassment should receive immediate attention and be reported to the EEO Coordinator. Investigations will be conducted in cooperation with the EEO Coordinator and may include conferring with parties and witnesses named by the complaining employee. Because of the sensitive nature of such complaints, incidents must be investigated with particular care and should remain, to the extent possible, strictly confidential.

Sanctions

If the investigation reveals that the complaint is valid, prompt action, sufficient to stop the harassment immediately and to prevent its recurrence, will be taken. This may include disciplinary action up to and including discharge. Should the investigation reveal that an employee has become the victim of harassment by a nonemployee, it will be the responsibility of the EEO Coordinator to take the appropriate action in dealing with the vendor, contractor or other employer of the person involved.

Designated Counselors are the Following Persons:
(list the names of the designated counselors)

Sexual Harassment: Policy 2

It is the policy of this organization that all employees be able to work in an environment free from all forms of discrimination—this includes sexual harassment.

Sexual harassment refers to behavior that is unwelcome, personally offensive, debilitates morale and interferes with work effectiveness.

The Equal Employment Opportunity Commission (EEOC) has adopted written guidelines stating that any sexual harassment tolerated by employers constitutes a violation of Title VII of the Civil Rights Act of 1964. The EEOC guidelines state:

> "Unwelcome sexual advances, requests for sexual favors, and other verbal or physical conduct of a sexual nature constitute sexual harassment when (1) submission to such conduct is made either explicitly or implicitly a term or condition of an individual's employment, (2) submission to or rejection of such conduct by an individual is used as the basis for employment decisions affecting such individual, or (3) such conduct has the purpose or effect of substantially interfering with an individual's work performance or creating an intimidating, hostile, or offensive working environment."

Violation of this rule will be the basis for appropriate discipline, up to and including termination.

It is the responsibility of each member of management to provide the necessary support to ensure that discrimination in employment does not occur and that associates are assured of a workplace free from sexual harassment.

All members of management should be advised of this policy and are accountable for its effective administration throughout their respective organizations.

All associates are encouraged to bring violations of this policy to the attention of the personnel department or their management promptly. Should a manager or supervisor be advised of an infraction of this policy, he/she should immediately report the incident to the personnel corporate office or the Manager of Employee Relations.

SAMPLE POLICIES (continued)

Sexual Harassment Policy 3
Sample Policy for All Employees

It is the Company's policy to prohibit harassment of one employee by another employee or supervisor on the basis of sex. While it is not easy to define precisely what harassment is, it certainly includes unwelcome sexual advances, requests for sexual favors and other verbal or physical conduct of a sexual nature, such as uninvited touching or sexually related comments. Any employee who feels that he or she is a victim of sexual harassment should immediately report the matter to _____.
Violations of this policy will not be tolerated and may result in discipline up to and including discharge.

Sexual Harassment Policy 4
Sample Policy for Supervisors

It is the Company's policy to prohibit harassment of one employee by another on the basis of sex. While it is not easy to define precisely what harassment is, it certainly includes unwelcome sexual advances, requests for sexual favors and other verbal or physical conduct of a sexual nature, such as uninvited touching or sexually related comments.

All members of management should be advised of this policy and held accountable for the effective administration of its intent throughout their respective organizations. Should a manager or supervisor be advised of an infraction of this policy, he/she should immediately report the incident to

_____.

Violations of this policy will not be tolerated and may result in discipline up to and including discharge.

IMPLEMENTING A SEXUAL HARASSMENT POLICY

Several steps are required to accomplish effective implementation of a sexual harassment policy.

- Communication
- Training
- Counseling

Test Your Knowledge

1. Where can you find a copy of your organization's sexual harassment policy?

_____

2. It is prominently displayed in the following locations:

_____

_____

3. _____ times a year, I discuss organizational personnel policies, including sexual harassment, with those who report to me.

4. If an employee in my organization wants to report that he/she has been sexually harassed, the procedure they would follow is:

_____

_____

_____

5. My personal responsibilities regarding sexual harassment are:

_____

_____

_____

COMMUNICATING THE SEXUAL HARASSMENT POLICY

The best policy is useless if it is not communicated effectively. Even if the organization already has a well-written policy, it is important to publicize it regularly through:

- **Permanent posting on bulletin boards**

- **Memos**

- **Articles in the organization's internal publications**

- **Meetings**

- **Training**

The best strategy is to use all these methods at various times throughout the year.

PERMANENT POSTING

The customary and most logical place to post the policy is on the same bulletin boards with EEO, Occupational Safety and Health Administration and other policy information.

MEMOS

When implementing a new sexual harassment policy, disseminate it throughout the organization, accompanied by an appropriate memo emphasizing its importance and stating that the organization will not tolerate harassment. If a policy is already in place, distribute a reminder memo at least once a year.

ARTICLES

Several approaches can be taken with an article.

- In a general article discussing positive work environments, positive interpersonal relations at work, including sexual harassment, fairness and gender and cultural differences

- In an article specifically addressing sexual harassment and its negative effects on both individuals and the organization, reiterate the organization's policy and procedures to address complaints

- As part of an article discussing EEO, discuss affirmative action and discrimination, including sexual harassment.

Effective articles establish a tone that informs rather than alienates. Sexual harassment, equal employment and affirmative action are sensitive topics. People often see sexual harassment as an issue only for overly sensitive females. An effective article with data and facts, which demonstrates the extent of harassment and its negative effects and costs, monetary and otherwise, for the victim, the harasser and the organization, can be a very useful tool against harassment.

MEETINGS

For new employees, both nonmanagement and management, orientation should cover the organization's human resource policies and procedures, including the sexual harassment policy. Managers should review and discuss the organization's policies and procedures on a routine basis in their department meetings. This makes it easy to address sexual harassment without overly emphasizing it.

No employee at any level should be able to claim ignorance of a policy as an excuse for an inappropriate behavior.

TRAINING

Education is necessary for prevention of sexual harassment and for the effective handling of complaints when they occur.

WHY TRAINING?

Review the EEOC *Guidelines on Sexual Harassment* on page 19. Now check situations below that you think would be considered sexual harassment. After you complete this exercise, turn to page 114 for the authors' analysis.

☐ Person A repeatedly requests a date, even though Person B declines every invitation and makes it clear he/she is not interested.

☐ A male supervisor looks women up and down while he is having a conversation with them.

☐ A female worker wears tight miniskirts to work which provokes some of her male co-workers to make sexual comments and jokes about her.

☐ A male employee hangs a calendar with nude pictures on the wall of his private office. A female co-worker is offended when she goes into his office to pick up a report from his desk.

☐ A female supervisor asks a male subordinate to work late and have dinner with her. At dinner, she makes repeated comments with sexual overtones, which makes him uncomfortable.

☐ A supervisor and staff of three men and two women have lunch to celebrate a staff member's birthday. One of the men tells a joke with sexual overtones. Everyone laughs except one of the women, who is quite offended. When she says so, everyone tells her she is too sensitive and is ruining their fun.

☐ A male vice president's female secretary declines an invitation by a major male client to go out for coffee. The client repeats the request and she declines again. The client complains to the vice president that the secretary is too touchy, unfriendly and not good for business.

☐ A female manager has an opening in her department. Three qualified individuals apply, including a male whom she used to date. She hires one of the women whom she believes will be the best with clients. The man complains to the manager's boss that his not being hired is sexual harassment because of their past relationship.

Some of these situations are complex. For example, in the third situation who is the harasser—the woman with the tight, short skirt or the men, or both?

Are women responsible if they wear suggestive clothing and flirt and then men make overtures and remarks? What if that woman is raped? Is she responsible then? And when is clothing or behavior suggestive and by whose definition?

Would you view these situations differently if the gender of the individuals were switched? What if the individuals were of the same sex, but nothing else changed?

What if an office of both men and women works well with a lot of joking and occasional sexual banter, but one person finds it offensive?

Will strict enforcement of a sexual harassment policy suppress all fun at work?

THOUGHTS AND FEELINGS

Reread the previous page. How do you personally feel and think about the questions raised?

Is a woman responsible when she wears suggestive clothing or flirts?

_____

_____

_____

What do you consider suggestive?

_____

_____

_____

How do you feel about flirting by men or women at work?

_____

_____

_____

How do you feel about jokes with sexual overtones and remarks in the workplace?

_____

_____

_____

How would you see these situations if the gender of the persons was reversed?

_____

_____

_____

THE TRAINING PROGRAM

Unless you are a very unusual person, this book will make you increasingly aware of the complexities and subtleties of confronting and preventing harassment. Because of this complexity and the differences in what individuals consider sexual harassment, training is crucial for both prevention and dealing effectively with sexual harassment complaints when they occur.

The steps in designing and implementing a comprehensive training program are:

- **Conduct a sexual harassment audit/attitude survey**

- **Design training**

- **Implement the training**

- **Evaluate the program**

For broad organizational problem solving and ownership of outcomes, your organization may wish to create a task force, which would include individuals from various backgrounds and organizational levels. This task force can be designated to address sexual harassment only, or broader interpersonal concerns and issues.

THE AUDIT

It is not recommended that an organization rush out suddenly, with no forewarning, and ask every individual about sexual harassment. But there are effective and efficient ways to find out how pervasive harassment is and where it may be occurring. These same strategies can be used to discover other discriminatory and inappropriate interpersonal behavior throughout the organization.

Policy, Procedure and Management Style Review

The audit should begin with a review of all human resource policies, procedures and practices, including management styles. To be effective, this review must answer the following questions.

1. Are policies and procedures clearly stated? Will they enable everyone in the organization to know exactly what is acceptable and unacceptable behavior? Is it clear what one must do to address a problem or issue a complaint?

_____

_____

_____

_____

_____

2. Does management live the policies and procedures, or merely give them lip service? How do you know?

_____

_____

_____

_____

_____

3. Do individuals feel they can address problems and file complaints without repercussion? How do you know?

_____

_____

_____

_____

_____

4. When an investigation occurs, how is privacy honored?

_____

_____

_____

_____

_____

5. Are investigations handled consistently and fairly, regardless of the organizational level of the individuals involved? How do you know this?

_____

_____

_____

_____

_____

THE AUDIT (continued)

Review of Terminations

An organization may have a few honest people who, in the termination interview, will tell you they are leaving because of harassment. Do not count on it. For a more accurate search:

► Analyze termination data. Is turnover higher in certain areas or departments or under a particular manager? Why?

► Review unemployment compensation filings. Sexual harassment may surface as a reason.

If terminations are higher in certain areas, an investigation may be appropriate. Patterns usually exist, particularly in cases where a supervisor or manager is the harasser.

Review of Organization Structure

Sexual harassment is harder to detect in autocratic, pyramidal organizational structures with narrowly defined jobs than it is in matrix organizations. This is true whether the harasser is the supervisor or another employee. Why?

Harassment can remain hidden within a department because communication is primarily vertical and formal rather than across departments. The extensive coordination and relating among departments that occurs in matrix organizations makes hiding any problem or issue difficult.

Review of Human Resources

The manner in which the human resources operation functions can have a dramatic effect on organizational attitudes toward equality, sexual harassment and relationships among organizational members. Several areas deserve special scrutiny.

► Recruitment and selection policies and practices

► The performance evaluation and management system

► Training

When reviewing recruitment and selection policies, procedures and practices, ask:

► Are these policies and practices unbiased and nondiscriminatory?

► Is selection based on more than one person's decision and on well-defined criteria?

The organization may want to pay special attention to practices in remote locations and field operations where inappropriate practices and behavior can easily occur undetected.

Human resources should review all individual evaluations with *below satisfactory* ratings to verify that such a rating is deserved. The following questions will assist in making such a determination.

► What was the individual's previous performance?

► Have there been previous performance problems in the same department or area? If so, is there any pattern?

► Does the supervisor have sufficient and appropriate documentation?

► What type of improvement plan has been initiated and was it mutually agreed upon?

Effective and routine monitoring of appraisals can be an excellent tool for the early detection of a problem.

THE AUDIT (continued)

Reinforcement

It has long been known, both in psychological circles and in performance management practice, that people continue or eliminate behaviors depending on the kinds of reinforcement they receive.

Observe your organization.

What kinds of attitudes and behavior patterns are reinforced?

_____

_____

_____

_____

_____

In meetings where the attendees are predominantly male, what kinds of jokes and remarks are made that might make a woman feel unwanted or harassed?

_____

_____

_____

_____

How do women treat men in a predominantly female department?

_____

_____

_____

_____

How do people in your organization talk about gays and lesbians?

_____

_____

_____

_____

_____

Do women receive equal pay? How do you know? How many women are in middle and upper management jobs?

_____

_____

_____

_____

_____

How do men talk about women in the organization when they are not present?

_____

_____

_____

_____

And vice versa?

_____

_____

_____

_____

THE AUDIT (continued)

The final question is especially important because the real culture and environment of an organization is generally established informally behind closed doors. This includes setting examples. Individuals in lower ranks tend to model the behavior of higher ranking, successful people.

What behaviors do your organization's executives model?

_____

_____

_____

_____

_____

When claims of sexual harassment are raised, the manner in which everyone involved is treated can either encourage harassment or deter it. Furthermore, how the complaint is handled may either encourage or discourage others from coming forward in the future. If those who complain have been branded as troublemakers in the past, the organization may have harassment going on and not even be aware of it because people are afraid to complain.

What You Can Do

Depending upon your position in the organization, you may not be able to answer all the questions or address the issues in this audit. Nevertheless, you can be a model for others and you can share this book with those who can affect policies, procedures and practices in the organization. No one is powerless. Each individual in an organization affects the total culture and environment.

PERSONAL AUDIT

PERSONAL AUDIT

Audit yourself:

How do you relate to others in your department and in the organization? Do you treat people differently depending on their gender or sexual orientation?

_____

_____

_____

_____

_____

What jokes or comments have you made that someone might consider sexual harassment?

_____

_____

_____

_____

_____

How do you know they did or did not feel harassed?

_____

_____

_____

When someone makes a joke or comment that you consider inappropriate or harassing, you . . .

_____

_____

_____

_____

_____

PERSONAL AUDIT (continued)

If you supervise others, go back to page 46, Thoughts and Feelings, and review your answers. Now go over the organizational audit questions and apply the questions to your area or department only.

How do people under your supervision know about organizational policies and procedures?

_____
_____
_____
_____

When was the last time someone in your department complained about a concern or issue? How did you handle it?

_____
_____
_____
_____

How do you know you handle situations honestly and consistently?

_____
_____
_____
_____

What is the turnover rate in your area?

_____
_____
_____
_____

Why did people leave?

_____

_____

_____

When you hire a new person, what criteria do you use for selection?

_____

_____

_____

When you last hired a new person, would it have made a difference if the person were of a different gender?

_____

_____

How do you know?

_____

_____

If someone from outside your area interviewed your employees regarding your management practices, how would those you supervise describe you?

_____

_____

_____

Now return to the questions on Reinforcement on pages 52 and 53. How would you change the answers if they applied only to you and your department?

_____

_____

_____

DESIGNING THE TRAINING

There are several training options.

► A specific program based on needs as determined from the information acquired in the audit

► Part of a general management skills program that includes a segment on sexual harassment

► A separate sexual harassment program

► Combination of some of the above

The organization must decide whether to use prepackaged material or develop its own. One effective option is to use ready-made audio-visual material as part of an overall program designed to meet specific organizational needs.

Effective training is conducted initially in the classroom, and includes continuous on-the-job feedback and development. The ultimate goal is to give individuals support, training and reinforcement to develop and consistently use effective interpersonal skills with all people, regardless of gender, ethnic origin and other differences.

At a minimum, effective sexual harassment classroom training must:

• Cover basic information on federal and state laws and major court cases (see pages 7–11)

• Include examples of effective and appropriate behavior for handling various situations

• Provide the opportunity to review and discuss complex case studies and examples

• Provide the opportunity to practice appropriate interpersonal skills in challenging situations

CASE STUDY #1

CASE STUDY
XYZ Corporation

Alex Jordan worked for the XYZ Corporation for many years. When he started working in the warehouse, all they made were boxes and other kinds of containers. For the last five years he has managed three warehouses and a large distribution network. He has a large staff, mostly of clerks, inventory people, warehouse workers and drivers. Until the last few years, almost everyone working for him has been male. Now he has two female clerks, one female driver and two women working in one of the warehouses. On the whole, he thinks the men reacted well to having women around. At first, there was some teasing and joking, but it did not last long. He thought everything was going smoothly, until about six months ago.

James Roachman is a new driver. He has an excellent record from his previous jobs, is tall, strong and clean-cut looking, just the sort of all-American fellow Alex feels comfortable with. Two months ago, one of the other drivers, George Strong, overheard a telephone conversation between James and another individual. From the words and tone of the conversation, the two were obviously intimate. George went to Alex very upset, because he was sure the other individual was a male. Alex told George it was none of his business and to go back to work.

It has not turned out to be that simple. Alex overheard George make negative comments about gays within James's hearing. At first, when James did nothing, Alex ignored it, hoping it would all go away. Instead, the negative comments increased. George started talking about James to others. Some of the other workers began avoiding James. Two days ago James came to Alex complaining that someone had left a threatening note on the seat of his truck. He threatened to go to the Civil Rights Commission to complain of sexual harassment. George promised to do something. However, two days have passed and he has done nothing. He feels extremely uncomfortable about the situation and does not know what to say or do about it.

TURN THE PAGE

IS THIS SEXUAL HARASSMENT?

Write your responses to the XYZ Case in the space provided. See the discussion on page 115.

1. Is this case an example of sexual harassment? Why or why not?

_____

_____

_____

_____

2. What should Alex do?

_____

_____

_____

_____

3. If James goes to the EEOC or a state agency, what will be the general procedure?

_____

_____

_____

_____

4. Which of your organization's policies and procedures would apply in a situation like this?

_____

_____

_____

_____

TRAINING IMPLEMENTATION— SETTING THE TONE

Executives, management and nonmanagement staff should all be trained to spot and handle instances of discrimination. There is nothing that sets a more negative tone than for lower level employees to discover that senior executives and management have not gone through training. Obviously, the training will not be identical for all individuals, at all levels.

Executives need only look throughout the lower ranks of an organization to see and hear their own behaviors. Executive's behavior has the greatest impact on the behavior of all others in the organization. They set the tone and others follow.

What is the official executive position regarding sexual harassment in your organization?

_____

_____

_____

Cite a circumstance or situation where you either saw or heard an executive in your organization engage in behavior that might be interpreted as harassment?

_____

_____

_____

What is the informal attitude in your organization toward sexual harassment?

_____

_____

_____

TRAINING IMPLEMENTATION—SETTING THE TONE (continued)

How does this differ from the formal policy?

_____

_____

_____

To merge the formal policies and informal practices and set an organizational tone where sexual harassment is not and will not be tolerated, the key executives of the organization must make it known they and the organization will not tolerate such behavior.

Communication of this can be part of the introductory training or orientation material or sent separately to all organizational members in a memo introducing the training. The task force can help decide which would be more appropriate and effective.

Ideally, any training program that includes sexual harassment should be mandatory for _every_ person working for the company. Otherwise, those who _need_ it most will not attend.

Generally, it will take at least one half day to cover laws, policies and procedures, and give examples of effective behavior. Another half day can be devoted to case studies and discussions, with practice on handling difficult situations. Managers will also need training on how to handle complaints, both procedurally and emotionally.

EVALUATION

The organization has set policies and procedures, completed an audit and implemented training. How do they know if it is working?

The effectiveness of any system is dependent on continual feedback and readjustment. After training, reask the initial audit questions. Have situations improved? Have new problems arisen? What adjustments need to be made to training in policies, procedures and practices? This never-ending process is crucial for effectiveness.

COUNSELING

Sally Smith, a 40-year-old analyst in Y department, comes into your office, looking very nervous and upset. She seems to be on the verge of tears. You ask her to sit down and inquire about the problem. With difficulty, she tells you that she feels she has been sexually harassed by the vice president over Y.

She claims he asked her out several times and she always made up excuses why she could not go. Lately, he has come into her office, brushed against her, and made remarks about her uncooperativeness. She says she did not come to you before because she was embarrassed and afraid; after all, he is a vice president. She asks you what she should do. She says she cannot take his attitude and actions any longer and has thought about quitting, but needs the job to take care of her two children and herself. She is a divorced single parent.

Describe how you would handle this situation. See the discussion on page 116.

_____

_____

_____

_____

_____

_____

_____

_____

_____

_____

If Sally were Sam, a male, what would be your reaction?

_____

_____

_____

How an organization deals with individuals who feel they have been harassed greatly affects the legitimacy of the organization's sexual harassment policies and procedures. The emotional aftereffects of any kind of harassment and abuse are strong and include feelings of loss and grief, anger and depression. Guilt and self-blame are particularly detrimental to the recovery process.

Rarely will a manager or human resources professional possess the expertise to provide in-depth counseling. Even if the individual appears to be emotionally sound, it is advisable to suggest referral sources. If the organization has an employee assistance program, suggest that the person may wish to talk with someone there.

When an individual comes to you with a complaint of sexual harassment:

- Be supportive and empathetic
- Carefully explain the procedures that will be followed
- Emphasize that the complaint is serious and will be handled as such
- Explain that separate counseling is available and where to find it

Letting the individual know that the situation will be thoroughly investigated, privately and discreetly, is very important psychologically as well as legally. Victims are often afraid to speak out because they feel their jobs may be in jeopardy, and because they fear an invasion of privacy.

If you are not the appropriate person to investigate the complaint, explain the procedure. Offer to initiate the process.

Cultural Considerations

Persons from different cultures may react very differently to sexual harassment. Some may not be inclined to pursue the matter. Some may not understand the law and their rights. Some may not speak the language. Organizations need to be sensitive to the difficulties their employees face in coming forward with a complaint and having that complaint resolved.

PRIVACY ISSUES

Like any sensitive interpersonal situation, sexual harassment complaints *must* be handled with utmost privacy. If not, individuals will be exceedingly reluctant to come forward and to discuss the situation with anyone in the organization. Handling of complaints internally is far preferable to the individual first seeking outside help.

Your organization should have a procedure for handling all complaints, not just those involving sexual harassment. This procedure should guarantee maximum privacy for the complaining party while allowing for necessary investigative activities.

In a union environment, this procedure may be called a grievance procedure. Regardless of its title, the procedure should:

- Be clear and easy to understand

- Be step-by-step so that everyone knows exactly what will happen and when

- Emphasize that all problems and investigations will be handled discreetly

Generally speaking, complaints should be addressed initially to the individual's immediate supervisor unless that person is the problem. This option should be well publicized to encourage employees to raise the issue. In sexual harassment situations, it is also advisable to involve human resources/employee relations immediately.

Consider the following:

Helen Thomas, a young employee, new to the organization, comes to your office. You supervise an area that works with her department. She tells you that another employee in her area has been harassing her, leaving suggestive notes and cartoons on her desk. She tells you she can handle the situation and does not want you to tell her supervisor or to involve human resources.

Should you respect her request for privacy and do nothing?

_____

_____

_____

What problems do you create for the organization if you do nothing, as she requested?

_____

_____

_____

Do you think the situation is more dangerous if you are a human resources manager?

_____

_____

_____

Because of the manner in which the agencies and courts have interpreted the EEOC guidelines, you have a responsibility to report the situation even if the employee requests that you do nothing. If, as a supervisor, you know about a harassment situation and take no remedial steps, the organization can be found legally liable. If you are the human resources manager and do nothing, the courts will not understand your lack of action. Once you, as a manager, know about the situation, it must be investigated and, if the facts show sexual harassment is occurring, remedial steps must be taken.

Therefore, you will have to tell the complainant that, although you understand his or her privacy concerns, you have an obligation to act. You should explain:

- Legal concerns .

- That others may be affected

- That, unstopped, sexual harassment can spread and more broadly infect the workplace

P A R T

IV

Handling Sexual Harassment Complaints

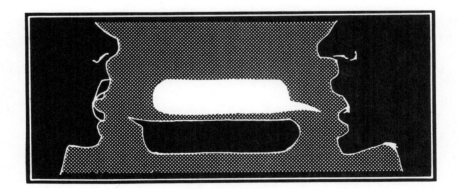

YOUR ORGANIZATION: A CHECKLIST

Courts today are taking a strong position with regard to claims of sexual harassment. Because of this, it is important that all supervisors, managers and employers are educated about sexual harassment claims.

What steps has your company taken to ensure that sexual harassment does not occur in the workplace?

	Yes	No
1. Does your organization offer regular training sessions to educate all employees about the implications of sexual harassment?	☐	☐
2. Has your organization appointed at least one representative to receive and investigate complaints of sexual harassment?	☐	☐
3. Is your organization representative a female?	☐	☐
4. Does your organization have two representatives, one male and one female, to receive and investigate complaints of sexual harassment?	☐	☐
5. Can an employee be terminated if found to have violated the organization's sexual harassment policy?	☐	☐
6. Does your organization maintain confidentiality when investigating complaints of sexual harassment?	☐	☐
7. Are victims of sexual harassment in your workplace involved in the decision as to appropriate corrective action to be taken?	☐	☐
8. If the complaint of sexual harassment is confirmed, are the terms and conditions of the employee altered; i.e., is the victim moved to another work area while the harasser is left where he/she was?	☐	☐

If your answer to No. 8 is yes, do you know why this is done? Would you agree that the victim is again being victimized? What alternatives does the organization have? _____

_____

The courts look at all the facts to determine if sexual harassment occurred and to determine the appropriate damages. The steps the employer takes with regard to the accused and the victim are important issues in that process.

SEXUAL HARASSMENT POLICY

The courts and the agencies investigating complaints of sexual harassment look at what the Equal Employment Opportunity Commission calls *the totality of the circumstances* to determine if sexual harassment has occurred. The process includes identifying the steps the organization has taken to address the problem.

The courts always ask if the organization has a policy prohibiting sexual harassment. Pages 37–40 include four sample policies against sexual harassment. The first is a broad policy prohibiting all types of harassment in the workplace; the others specifically address sexual harassment. The policy you decide to use should be posted or appear in the employee handbook, should be permanently displayed on your organization's bulletin boards and should appear in the organization's policy manual.

Your organization's legal department or an outside attorney should review the policy to ensure that it does not create any unknown or unintended obligations for the organization.

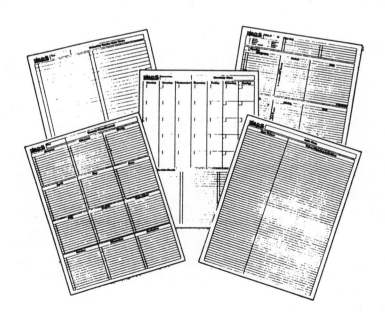

CHOOSING THE RIGHT PERSON

It is not enough for an organization to have a policy against sexual harassment; it must take steps to demonstrate to its employees that the policy is important. The first step is to choose one or two people to accept and investigate complaints of sexual harassment. What attributes would you look for in making this choice? List the attributes below:

_____

_____

_____

_____

_____

_____

_____

_____

_____

_____

_____

	Yes	No
Would it matter if the person(s) you choose are male or female?	☐	☐
Would women be more likely to bring their complaints to other women?	☐	☐
Should the person appointed be one of the supervisors or an owner of the organization?	☐	☐
Should the person appointed have been a victim of sexual harassment?	☐	☐
Should the person considered for the job have any specialized training?	☐	☐

THE IN-HOUSE INVESTIGATION FOLLOWING A COMPLAINT

All investigations of claims of discrimination should be kept confidential. In part, this is because antidiscrimination laws prohibit retaliating against a claimant who exercises his/her rights to raise the claim. Potential libel or slander actions by the accused are other factors to be considered.

Although the investigation should be handled in a confidential manner, some matters cannot always be kept confidential. Consider the following situation.

> You receive a complaint of sexual harassment by an employee who claims some of her male co-workers have made offensive jokes with sexual innuendoes in her presence. She asked them to stop. She claims one of the co-workers even brought an ''X'' rated video to the office. He told her to take it home, watch it and think of him. She is afraid that if her co-workers know she has complained they will make working in the area even more difficult. She is not the only female in the area.

You may be able to conduct the necessary interviews without revealing the name of the complainant. Questions can be phrased in terms of what goes on in the workplace on an ongoing basis, rather than ''Did you tell a dirty joke while Jane was in the office?''

For example: ''Do you joke around?'' ''Does everyone participate in the banter?'' ''What kind of jokes are told?'' ''Does everyone tell jokes?'' ''Does the supervisor participate too?'' Has anyone ever asked that the jokes stop?''

DUTIES OF THE INVESTIGATOR OF SEXUAL HARASSMENT CLAIMS

The individual conducting the investigation needs to be knowledgeable about the organization and its employees. She/he needs to be familiar with good investigative techniques, including interviewing and reviewing of documentation. She/he should also be well respected by all levels of the organization. Why do you think this last issue is important?

_____

_____

_____

_____

_____

_____

In investigating the complaint, the investigator should:

- Make certain she/he understands the complaint

- Interview complainant and get all facts before doing any other investigations

- Interview all possible witnesses—co-workers, supervisors, customers

- Interview the accused

- Gather all relevant documentation

- Make a report on the investigation

- If appropriate, make recommendation for action

DOCUMENTATION PROCEDURES

Because of the complexity of the issues involved in claims of sexual harassment, it is important that supervisors and managers utilize good documentation techniques in investigating claims.

Documentation should include:

☐ Interviews with witnesses, dated and signed by the investigator. Statements should be signed and dated by the witnesses.

☐ Relevant documents concerning the victim include:

1. Employment application

2. Reference checks

3. Evaluations for the entire employment period with the organization

4. Disciplinary warnings for all persons involved

5. Other memos concerning wage matters and promotions

☐ Documentation of any similar cases.

What other documentation should be collected during the in-house investigation?

_____

_____

_____

_____

_____

_____

_____

_____

To ensure confidentiality, if the organization works regularly with a law firm, you may want to have that firm conduct the investigation.

INTERVIEW OF COMPLAINANT

When an employee complains of sexual harassment, the wise employer takes the complaint seriously. If you do not, a union organizer or plaintiff's attorney might. The investigation may ultimately reveal that sexual harassment did not occur, but an investigation that includes an interview with the complainant should be initiated. This interview must be handled carefully.

What questions would you ask? How many people would you think should be present? Should the interview be taped?

List five questions you would ask if you were conducting the interview:

1. _____

_____

2. _____

_____

3. _____

_____

4. _____

_____

5. _____

_____

INTERVIEW OF COMPLAINANT (continued)

In your responses on page 77, did you include:

1. When did the sexual harassment occur? How long ago?

2. Over how long a period of time did the sexual harassment take place?

3. Did the sexual harassment happen at the office, the plant, a restaurant, the complainant's or harasser's home?

4. Did the complainant ever tell the accused to stop bothering him/her, or reject the advances in any way? If not, why not?

5. If several weeks or months have passed since the sexual harassment occurred, find out why the complainant waited so long to report the harassment.

6. Identify names of witnesses, what they witnessed, and if the complainant has discussed the claim with the witnesses.

7. Gather any other corroborating documentation of harassment.

8. Does the complainant have notes, letters or other documentation he/she claims was authored by the accused? If the complainant does have such documentation, you will want to see it and make copies.

What other questions do you feel would be appropriate?

_____

_____

_____

_____

The complainant should be interviewed by one company representative. Although it might help to have two company representatives present at the interview, the employee, who is probably already the victim of some kind of intimidation, may be further intimidated.

If you are not a good note taker, tape the interview. Inform the person that the interview will be taped and explain that you will use the tape recorder to ensure accuracy.

INTERVIEWING THE ACCUSED

Because the organization cares about its employees as well as potentially expensive lawsuits, the interview of the accused harasser must also be handled carefully. Although many females and males have been victims of sexual harassment, occasionally an employee will use a sexual harassment complaint to mask the real reason for a termination, demotion or being passed over for a new job. The concept of *not guilty unless proven otherwise* must be remembered during the interview of the accused. You do not want to be faced with a libel or slander lawsuit by the accused.

Test Your Knowledge

In addition to the precautions necessary when interviewing the complainant, can you think of other things you should keep in mind when interviewing the accused?

_____

_____

_____

_____

_____

_____

_____

_____

_____

_____

_____

_____

INTERVIEWING THE WITNESSES

Unless other persons claim to have been harassed by the accused, the organization may find it difficult, if not impossible, to determine if sexual harassment occurred.

In the majority of sexual harassment cases, the only people present, and therefore witness to the actions, are the *victim* and the *accused*. While there may have been other persons present in the work area, they have often not witnessed the alleged harassment.

Nevertheless, it is important for the organization to explore every area for facts and an understanding of what occurred. Persons in the work area should be interviewed. If you want to protect the accused as well as the victim, consider how you can conduct these interviews without revealing names.

How can you phrase interview questions to avoid potential slander actions by the accused who is later found to be innocent?

_____

_____

_____

_____

_____

_____

_____

_____

While questioning possible witnesses, questions should be as general as possible. Some examples are:

- Have you seen anything unusual in the area?

- Do all employees in this area get along?

- Is there a lot of exchanging of jokes?

REVIEW AND MAINTENANCE OF RECORDS

When the investigation is completed, place all documents in a separate file and keep them in a locked area in the personnel department.

Do not put them in the accused's personnel file or in the file of the person who is alleging the harassment. This is particularly true if the accused is later cleared of the charges.

RESOLVING THE COMPLAINT

You have interviewed all witnesses and collected a lot of documentation. You are of the opinion sexual harassment has occurred. What steps will you take to resolve this situation? Depending on the circumstances, the resolution of the complaint should include some or all of the following:

- Consult with the complainant concerning an appropriate way to resolve the matter

- If the employee was denied a promotion, consider placing the employee in the appropriate position

- If the complainant lost wages, consider payment of those lost wages, because if you do not, the complainant may obtain an agency or court order to be paid

- An employee who transferred out of his/her job should be given the option of returning to that job

- The accused should be terminated or issued a written warning.

As appropriate, prepare a settlement document, which should be reviewed by an attorney for the organization. The harassed employee should be permitted to have an attorney review the document.

We have been discussing situations where your investigation substantiates charges of sexual harassment. What happens if the investigation is inconclusive? Think about that for a moment.

You need to report the results of your investigation to the complainant as well as the accused. The report to the complainant must include:

- A statement that the investigation was inconclusive
- An inquiry as to whether she/he can still work in that area; if not, explore the possibility of a transfer to another area
- Counseling that if another incident occurs, it should be reported at once.

What else would you tell the employees involved? Speak with the employee who was accused. Emphasize that even though the investigation was inconclusive, any additional incidents will be investigated and, if substantiated, appropriate action, up to and including termination, will be taken.

If you follow the steps outlined in this section, the problem, at least for the moment, will have been remedied. However, if the employee subsequently retains a lawyer or seeks the assistance of an administrative agency, you have placed your organization in a defensible position.

PART

V

Governmental Agencies and the Courts

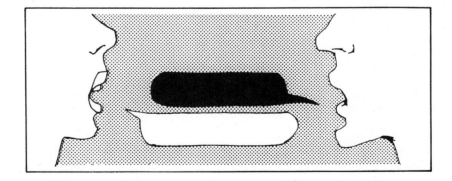

THE ROLE OF GOVERNMENTAL AGENCIES: THE CHARGE PROCESS

Although most employers today try to create an open atmosphere, often employees will not report sexual harassment to their supervisors or to human resources.

Have you considered why this might occur? Consider the following reasons given by persons who did not complain to their organization before filing an administrative charge or lawsuit:

► Concern about retaliation from the supervisor, manager or other co-employees

► Lack of faith in the organization's investigative process

► A belief that because they were already terminated, nothing positive would result from complaining to the organization

► Fear that other employees would learn about the complaint and gossip about it

► Concern that they might not find another job because they would be labeled as troublemakers

As a result of these concerns, employees often will seek assistance from persons outside of their organization. These outsiders include attorneys, federal and state administrative agencies charged with investigating discrimination claims and unions.

As we noted earlier, within the United States, the Equal Employment Opportunity Commission is the federal agency charged with investigating charges of sexual harassment.

In many states, the charge process is handled by a state agency or local administrative agency which works with the EEOC in what is called a work-sharing agreement. Due primarily to heavy caseloads, such an agency will normally be the one to investigate the charge.

THE ROLE OF GOVERNMENTAL AGENCIES: THE CHARGE PROCESS (continued)

What local or state agency in your area accepts and investigates complaints of discrimination?

_____

_____

Where in your area is it located?

_____

_____

Although every state or local agency handles the investigation of a charge of discrimination a little differently, the procedures followed by the federal agency are the same throughout the country. There is at least one office of the EEOC in every state; some states have several offices. Where is the EEOC in your state?

_____

Any individual who believes he/she has been sexually harassed can file a charge with the EEOC if the following requirements are met.

1. The charge must be timely; i.e., filed within 180 days of the alleged harassment, and

2. The complainant must be able to present what is called a _prima facie_ case of sexual harassment.

It costs nothing to file a charge of discrimination. The charge process can be initiated through a letter; a phone call will not usually be sufficient.

Even if the complainant cannot meet the above criteria, they can insist that charges be filed, and the agency must accept the charge. After the charge is filed, the law requires that it be served on the accused organization. This is usually done within 10 days after the charge is filed with the EEOC. From the time the charge is filed, it can take as little as one week or as long as several years for it to be resolved. The graph on the facing page shows the steps a charge of sexual harassment follows.

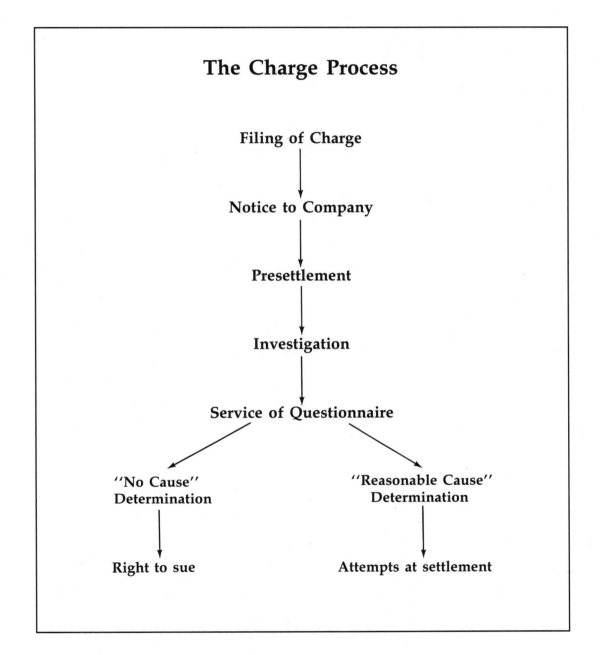

The Charge Process

Filing of Charge

Notice to Company

Presettlement

Investigation

Service of Questionnaire

"No Cause"
Determination

"Reasonable Cause"
Determination

Right to sue

Attempts at settlement

THE SETTLEMENT PROCESS— "FIRST BITE"

After a charge of sexual harassment has been filed, the agency investigating the charge often contacts the employer to determine if the charge can be settled before an investigation. A fast settlement may resolve the matter within weeks; an investigation can drag out over a year and the case will still not be resolved.

List five reasons why an employer might consider settling a charge of sexual harassment before it has been determined that it even occurred.

1. _____

_____

2. _____

_____

3. _____

_____

4. _____

_____

5. _____

_____

Did you include the following?

• To save costs associated with a lengthy investigation, including attorney's fees and the cost to pull managers away from work

• To avoid an investigation by a state or federal agency, which might uncover other problems

• For employee relations reasons; i.e., the impact of having outsiders on the worksite

• A settle-all-problems attitude

• Knowledge that the harassment did occur

What are some other reasons?

_____

_____

_____

_____

What are some reasons why an employer might decide not to settle a sexual harassment charge at this stage?

_____

_____

_____

_____

The agencies know employers will take all of these into consideration in deciding if settlement is appropriate at this stage.

If an employer believes that sexual harassment has occurred, it should consider settling the case early in the charge process. The settlement may include a monetary award, development and publication of a sexual harassment policy if none exists and discipline of the accused, including possible suspension, loss of wages and termination of employment.

In settling a claim, the agency may want to use only its own settlement documents, which resolve the charge before the agency. An organization should consider employing a broad settlement document, ensuring that all possible claims of the employee are resolved—for example, possible tort and contract claims.

Following is some sample language.

THE SETTLEMENT PROCESS—"FIRST BITE" (continued)

AGREEMENT

1. The Organization shall pay Employee the gross sum of $_____ (less all normal and usual deductions for taxes and benefits) in settlement of any and all potential claims Employee believes he/she may have against the Organization. If Employee has revoked the waiver and release of all rights to proceed against the Organization, this Agreement may be nullified at the option of the Organization and no money will be paid.

2. (Details concerning the payment by the Organization and other agreements by the Organization should be put in this section.)

3. This SETTLEMENT AGREEMENT AND GENERAL RELEASE is not and shall not in any way be construed as an admission by the Organization or any of its current or former employees of any wrongful or unlawful acts or of any breach of any agreement whatsoever. The parties have entered into this SETTLEMENT AGREEMENT AND GENERAL RELEASE for the sole purpose of resolving all claims that the Employee may have against the Organization in order to avoid the burden, expense, delay and uncertainties of litigation.

4. In consideration of the agreements and promises made by the Organization to Employee set forth in Paragraph 1 and 2 above, Employee thereby releases the Organization and all of its current and former employees and agents from all claims (including those under Title VII of the Civil Rights Act of 1964, as amended), liabilities, obligations, promises, agreements, controversies and damages of any nature and kind, known or unknown, attributable to or otherwise arising from any alleged conduct or practices by the Organization or any of its current or former employees or agents or otherwise related to Employee's employment relationship with the Organization or the termination thereof.

5. Employee further agrees, promises and covenants that neither Employee, nor any person acting on his/her behalf, will file any action for damages or relief (including injunctive, declaratory, monetary relief or other) against the Organization or any of its current or former employees or agents relating to any matter occurring in the past up to the date of this SETTLEMENT AGREEMENT AND GENERAL RELEASE or involving any continuing effects of actions and practices which arose prior to the date of this SETTLEMENT AGREEMENT AND GENERAL RELEASE, or

involving and based upon any claims, demands, causes of action, obligations, damages or liabilities which are the subject of this SETTLEMENT AGREEMENT AND GENERAL RELEASE.

6. Employee covenants and agrees that he/she will keep the terms, amount and fact of the agreements set forth in this SETTLEMENT AGREEMENT AND GENERAL RELEASE completely confidential, and that Employee will not hereinafter disclose any information concerning this SETTLEMENT AGREEMENT AND GENERAL RELEASE to any person other than his/her present attorneys.

7. Except as expressly provided below, neither Employee, his/her representatives, nor his/her attorneys shall make any statements to anyone (person, agency, entity, etc.) concerning the facts that relate to this settlement. If any person makes any inquiry of Employee, his/her attorneys, or any other representative of Employee that directly or indirectly relates to Organization, Employee, his/her attorneys, and representatives shall limit their response to a statement that all matters between Employee and the Organization have been resolved to the satisfaction of all parties. These provisions or restrictions shall not apply to any inquiry by a responsible governmental official or agency nor shall they apply to any instance in which Employee is required to provide testimony or give evidence in response to a lawful order of a court of competent jurisdiction or an administrative body which has subpoena power. This confidentiality provision is hereby specifically identified as material to this SETTLEMENT AGREEMENT AND GENERAL RELEASE and it is specifically agreed that a breach of this term by Employee, his/her attorneys or representatives shall constitute a breach of this SETTLEMENT AGREEMENT AND GENERAL RELEASE.

8. Employee represents and certifies that he/she has carefully read and fully understands all the provisions and effects of this SETTLEMENT AGREEMENT AND GENERAL RELEASE and has thoroughly discussed all aspects of this SETTLEMENT AGREEMENT AND GENERAL RELEASE with his/her private attorney, that Employee is voluntarily entering into this SETTLEMENT AGREEMENT AND GENERAL RELEASE, and that neither the Organization nor its agents, representatives or attorneys made any representations concerning the terms of effects of this SETTLEMENT AGREEMENT AND GENERAL RELEASE other than those contained herein in writing.

THE SETTLEMENT PROCESS—"FIRST BITE" (continued)

9. Should any provision of this SETTLEMENT AGREEMENT AND GENERAL RELEASE be declared or be determined by any Court to be illegal or invalid, the validity of the remaining parts, terms or provisions shall not be effected thereby and said illegal or invalid part, term or provision shall be deemed not part of this SETTLEMENT AGREEMENT AND GENERAL RELEASE.

10. This SETTLEMENT AGREEMENT AND GENERAL RELEASE sets forth the entire Agreement between the parties hereto and fully supersedes any and all prior agreements or understandings between the parties hereto pertaining to the subject matter hereof.

11. Employee understands and agrees that this SETTLEMENT AGREEMENT AND GENERAL RELEASE shall bind and benefit the heirs, employees, predecessors, subsidiaries, parents, agents, affiliates, attorneys and representatives of Employee and the Organization.

PLEASE READ CAREFULLY. THIS SETTLEMENT AGREEMENT AND GENERAL RELEASE INCLUDES A RELEASE OF ALL KNOWN AND UNKNOWN CLAIMS.

In WITNESS WHEREOF and intending to be legally bound hereby, Employee has executed the foregoing SETTLEMENT AGREEMENT AND GENERAL RELEASE.

Executed at _____ and _____ this _____ day of _____.

Witness: EMPLOYEE:

_____   _____

                                              _____

Note: If the charge is not settled at this stage, it will go forward to an investigation.

THE AGENCY INVESTIGATIVE PROCESS

A charge of sexual harassment is more difficult to investigate than other discrimination charges because most charges of sexual harassment come down to one person's word against another's. In addition to interviews of witnesses, what evidence will be necessary to resolve a charge of sexual harassment before an administrative agency? List three items you think would be requested by the agency.

1. _____

_____

2. _____

_____

3. _____

_____

After the agency sends a copy of the charge to the organization, it will forward a lengthy questionnaire. Consider limiting the response to that information which is relevant to the charge of sexual harassment. The information sent to an administrative agency may be ''discoverable'' if a case goes to court, that is, the information you reveal may be released to the plaintiff in a lawsuit. It may also be seen by other federal or state agencies. For these reasons, the response should be considered carefully. The organization's legal staff should be involved in preparation of the response to the administrative agency.

For example, if the charge is that the employee was not promoted because he/she did not participate in a sexual relationship with his/her boss, documents relevant to this charge would be:

1. Documents of other promotions or other types of personnel actions within the same department within the relevant time period; i.e., six months before or after the charge

THE INVESTIGATIVE PROCESS (continued)

2. Documents of other persons who applied for promotions but were denied the job within a relevant time period; i.e., six months before the charge was filed

3. A current EEO-1: a report completed by all employers with 100 or more employees, which shows how males/females and minorities are utilized within the organization

4. A list of all persons recommended for promotion by the supervisor within the relevant time period

5. Records of prior complaints by this employee or by other employees that involve this supervisor

6. Disciplinary records concerning the complaining employee

7. Disciplinary records concerning the alleged offender

8. A copy of the organization's sexual harassment policy as well as documentation of the steps the organization has taken to publicize it

9. A copy of the training manual or other appropriate training materials used by the organization to sensitize all employees to the issue of sexual harassment

10. If the organization investigated the charge and found no sexual harassment, the summary of the investigation may be relevant.

THE DETERMINATION

At the conclusion of its investigation, the EEOC normally issues a *Letter of Determination.* This is a letter which summarizes the findings of the agency, either that there is *no reasonable* or *no probable cause* to believe sexual harassment has occurred; or that there is *reasonable or probable cause* to believe sexual harassment has occurred. If a state agency has conducted the investigation, it may issue its own determination; if sufficient facts support doing so, EEOC will issue a complaint, taking the case to a hearing.

The issuance of a complaint normally means that a hearing before an administrative law judge will follow.

What weight do you think the courts give letters of determination?

_____

_____

_____

Some courts view the determination as closing the doors to any further litigation on the issue. Whether this occurs depends on how the investigative process was handled, the opportunity for both sides to cross examine witnesses, and the evidence. If the courts give the determination great weight, this may be termed *collateral estoppel.* Some courts may admit the determination into evidence, but give it little or no weight.

This is not the end of the process. If a *no cause* letter is issued, the agency will issue the complainant a letter known as a *Right to Sue,* which gives the complainant 90 days to file a lawsuit. At one time the courts were very liberal in appointing counsel to represent employees in discrimination cases. The courts have become much more restrictive in making such appointments. If the employee does not file his/her lawsuit within 90 days, this case is probably finished.

If the EEOC finds *cause* to believe sexual harassment has occurred, it will attempt to *conciliate* or settle the case. If the case is not settled, the agency is likely to file a lawsuit in federal court against the employer.

Often, if the complainant is represented by an attorney, the attorney will request authority to file a lawsuit in court. The agency must then give the complainant his/her *Right to Sue.* This may end involvement of the agency in the case.

THE SETTLEMENT PROCESS—SECOND TIME AROUND

After the agency has issued a letter of determination that sexual harassment has occurred, several things may occur.

► If an attorney represents the employee, the attorney may request authority or permission to file a lawsuit; this normally terminates the agency's involvement in the case

► The agency enters into settlement or conciliation to resolve the charge

► The agency decides to take the case to court or to a hearing on its own

If the case is closed before the agency at the request of the complainant's attorney, it is unlikely that it will be settled before suit has been filed. For this reason, the organization should seriously consider settlement of the case at this stage. Unlike a settlement at the start of the process, after a finding of discrimination, the agency will be looking for a remedy that makes the individual harassed *whole,* or puts the employee where she/he would have been had the harassment not occurred. At this stage, the stakes and costs are much higher. If the case is not settled at this juncture, it will go to court. There, as discussed earlier, the costs will quickly escalate.

THE COURTS

What should you do if notified that you or your organization has been charged with sexual harassment in a lawsuit?

_____

_____

_____

_____

_____

_____

Retaining Legal Assistance

If your organization is sued for sexual harassment in a state or federal court, you will want to be represented by an attorney who practices employment law. If your organization's attorney does not practice in this area, ask for a referral. Alternatively, you can contact your local bar association, which frequently has a lawyer referral panel. Because labor law is so complex, representation by counsel who has not previously handled such cases may be unnecessarily costly. This is true during the charge process as well as in court.

How the Courts Operate

Lawsuits alleging sexual harassment will include claims of personal injury, emotional distress and contract claims.

While previously a case brought under Title VII of the Civil Rights Act of 1964 could only be tried before a judge, recent changes in the law may permit a trial before a jury. Additionally, claims involving personal injury (assault, battery, intentional infliction of emotional distress, invasion of privacy) can be tried before a jury. Already an emotional and explosive issue, sexual harassment thus becomes extremely expensive, since juries are made up of men and women, who, if they have not been harassed themselves, may have friends or family who have been the victims of sexual harassment. Juries in such cases may award large judgments to plaintiffs.

THE COURTS (continued)

Once a case involving claims of sexual harassment is filed, a lengthy and expensive process begins. Depending on how heavy the court docket is, the case may come to trial in six months or five years. In the interim, a process known as discovery will occur. Discovery is the *learning* of the claims and damages and defenses of both sides. In this process, employees, managers and supervisors will be called on to answer questions, called interrogatories, and to testify under oath before a court reporter in depositions.

Anywhere in this process, settlement may occur. However if the complainant's attorney feels that their case is strong, settlement may be difficult or expensive.

Before the case is tried, a process called *summary judgment* may be undertaken. In summary judgment, one side argues to the court, through a legal document, that there is no dispute about the facts, and based on current law, the case should be decided prior to trial for either the employee or the organization.

Courts do not readily grant motions for summary judgment. Because there is often conflicting testimony in sexual harassment cases, courts hesitate to grant summary judgment. If summary judgment is denied, the case will be scheduled for trial.

PART

VI

Maintaining a Positive Work Environment

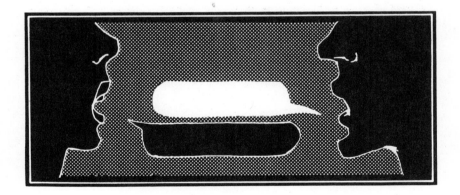

CREATING A POSITIVE INTERPERSONAL ENVIRONMENT

Everyone wants a secure, safe place to work. However, safety and security alone do not produce a positive environment or maximum productivity. Safety and security are what experts call *dissatisfiers*; i.e., if they are not there, people complain and productivity drops. Certainly safety and security elements are absent when sexual harassment occurs.

Creating a Positive Work Environment: Self-Test

List the positive qualities in your own work environment.

_____

_____

_____

List what is missing for you in your work environment.

_____

_____

_____

Do the positives outweigh what is missing?

_____

_____

If not, why are you working there?

_____

_____

_____

On an average day, what percentage of your time at work is enjoyable?

_____

_____

CREATING A POSITIVE INTERPERSONAL ENVIRONMENT (continued)

Look at the positives you listed and your "what's missing" list. Which list contains most of the interpersonal elements?

_____

Unless you are a very unusual person, a lot of how you feel about work is based on only a few things:

- Whether you like the work itself

- How well you get along with the people

- Whether you think you are making a contribution

Of these factors, which is most important to you?

_____

_____

_____

What do you do daily at work to make the environment positive?

_____

_____

_____

What behaviors have you engaged in at work that someone might consider sexual harassment?

_____

_____

_____

IF YOU DO NOT KNOW, FIND OUT AT ONCE!

Case Study—The Insurance Company

Georgia Wise was head of the systems accounting area at a large international insurance company. Most employees in her area had worked there with her for at least two years. It was a fun group with lots of teamwork. They were very busy, knew what needed to be accomplished and were great at putting their heads together and getting it done.

It was also a very relaxed atmosphere with a lot of bantering and joking, some of which was a bit sexual and contained a lot of innuendoes. It was fun, harmless teasing and no one seemed to care. No one, that is, until Georgia hired a young man, Tom, who had been able, due to his specialized expertise, to solve some problems the team had wrestled with for some time.

However, Tom seemed very serious and uncomfortable with the rest of the group. The staff consistently asked him to come with them to lunch or breaks, but he always declined. Some employees complained that he did not belong and interfered with the overall team spirit.

Recently, Georgia had been watching the interactions in the department more carefully to try to figure out what was going on. She noticed Sandra approach Tom several times and make remarks about how good he looked, joking and teasing a bit. Tom did not look very happy about it. Another time, Amid told a joke with sexual undertones. Tom was the only person who did not laugh.

CASE STUDY ANALYSIS

CASE STUDY ANALYSIS

Georgia did not want to endanger the fun teamwork that had been so effective in the past, but she had to do something about Tom. If you were Georgia, what would you do?

_____

_____

_____

_____

_____

_____

_____

What could Tom do, assuming he was uncomfortable about the sexual overtones of some of the jokes and banter?

_____

_____

_____

_____

_____

_____

_____

A harasser is a person with a sexual orientation toward relationships. No one expects people not to notice each other, how they look, their gender. That would be impossible. But noticing and abusing are not the same thing.

As men and women, and people of different ethnic origins, we are taught to be polite at work. We may be seething inside, but we say nothing. Sometimes we even smile and laugh and act as if nothing is wrong.

When we carry the politeness to this extreme, we are expecting the other person or persons to intuit that we do not like their behavior. It simply does not work that way, especially in the more subtle situation of sexual harassment. In this situation, everyone but Tom is happy with the work environment. Tom is miserable and it is beginning to affect everyone.

A poor solution: Tom might have stopped Sandra right in her tracks with some quick remark. Give an example of such a remark:

_____

_____

But such a remark only serves to escalate the situation and increase conflict. Sandra would think Tom is a jerk and tell everyone else. The entire department would be negatively affected.

An effective solution: Tom would politely tell Sandra he appreciated her compliments, but that they made him feel uncomfortable and he preferred she not repeat them. He could add that he thinks certain kinds of behavior are inappropriate in the office. Later, he could approach Amid, explaining that he feels like a spoil-sport mentioning the joke, but that he feels such jokes are out of place in the office. He could request that Amid not tell such jokes when he is around. To soften things, Tom could try to learn some jokes he thinks are appropriate.

Now, we will look at what Georgia can do. She can have a private talk with Tom, mention her observations and listen to his response. She can coach Tom on how to handle the situation. She can ask Tom for suggestions to keep the department friendly, fun and team spirited and still meet his needs for more decorum.

SAYING NO/STOPPING UNWELCOME BEHAVIOR

A lot of the subtle behavior that might be tagged harassment continues to occur because the *harasser* has never been told that his/her behavior is affecting others. At the same time, people seldom receive coaching or training on how to address conflict. When you speak up:

► Use "I" messages; e.g., "I feel uncomfortable when . . ."

► Avoid making smart remarks or quips

► Be ready for some response, possibly even anger

► Be prepared to tell the person what you want/need to keep a good relationship

► If this is not the first occurrence, explain why you said nothing previously; e.g., "I didn't want to offend you . . ."

► Be prepared to listen to the other person's side

Adhering to the above is of paramount importance when the person is a supervisor. Always concentrate on the behavior in question, not the person's character or personality.

This is not easy if you have never approached relationships in this manner before. Before you try it you may want to practice with a mirror or friends.

Experts note that sexual harassment often starts off in its milder forms and escalates because the *harasser* assumed there was no objection to the earlier behaviors. Therefore, it is extremely important that people speak up early.

A private, written note, repeating what was stated earlier in conversation may be appropriate. Privacy is the important thing at this stage. Then, if the inappropriate behavior ceases, the relationship can continue positively.

If you are responsible for training, create additional scenarios and have the trainees practice role playing the situations.

MAINTAINING A HARASSMENT-FREE WORKPLACE

Positive Impacts on Productivity

Frequently, organizations worry about sexual harassment costs from only the legal standpoint. This is a mistake. Take another look at the statistics on page 24 and the government study beginning on page 23. Sexual harassment costs are pervasive.

To be productive people have to:

- Feel safe and secure from overt physical and psychological harm

- Have good relationships with others with whom they work

- Feel respected for who they are and what they can contribute

Sexual harassment destroys all these criteria.

The training this book recommends has positive outcomes beyond preventing harassment:

- Builds teamwork

- Teaches people how to constructively resolve conflicts at home as well as at work

- Helps people gain new understanding and respect for each other and their differences

All these outcomes lead to improved productivity and organizational success.

**For additional training ideas and material, see the Crisp books, *Men and Women, Partners at Work* and *Working Together in a Multi-Cultural Organization.*

P A R T

VII

Solutions to Case Studies and Questions

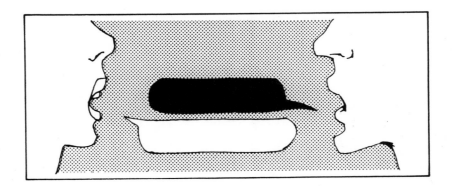

ANSWERS AND SOLUTIONS

Test Your Knowledge of Sexual Harassment (from page 2)

1. **False.** Sexual harassment is not an issue that concerns only one gender. Women and men have both been sexually harassed. There have also been instances where men have been sexually harassed by other men.

2. **False.** While it is important that all employers have a policy that prohibits sexual harassment in the workplace and prescribes discipline for violation of the policy, an employer must take other steps to ensure that sexual harassment does not occur. This includes training of all employees about sexual harassment, having in place an internal grievance mechanism that processes charges of sexual harassment, and investigating all charges of sexual harassment.

3. **False.** People need to enjoy coming to work. Limiting relationships between employees will not free an organization of sexual harassment. It may create an unfun place to be. An organization should ensure, however, that where supervisors and subordinates date, these relationships are free of sexual harassment. Your organization may want to consider implementing an affirmative action policy.

4. **False.** Although the U.S. Supreme Court in 1986 found sexual harassment based on an objective, gender-neutral reasonable person standard, several federal appellate courts have interpreted that standard as applicable to the reasonable woman.

5. **False.** According to a number of surveys, while situations of *quid pro quo* sexual harassment occur often in the workplace, instances of harassment that create an abusive or hostile environment occur more frequently.

6. **False.** See number 4 above.

Sexual Harassment in the Workplace

ANSWERS AND SOLUTIONS (continued)

7. **True.** A court can award damages for back pay, emotional harm, punitive damages and attorney fees to an injured employee in a sexual harassment case. There have been cases where the courts have prohibited the employer from paying the damages because of the injurious acts of sexual harassment.

8. **True.** This is a really difficult question. The EEOC Guidelines on sexual harassment say that where "employment is given to an employee because of his/her submission to the employer's request for sexual favors, the employer may be held liable for unlawful sexual discrimination against other persons who were qualified for but denied the employment opportunity or benefit." At least one court has coined the phrase *ugly discrimination* in describing this situation. It is clear that sexual harassment adversely affects not only the harassed employee, but others in the work area who are denied employment opportunities because of the harassment.

9. **False.**

10. **False.** Sexual harassment can be stopped if an organization takes a positive stand against sexual harassment by:

- Establishing a policy prohibiting sexual harassment in the workplace

- Publishing and posting the policy

- Training all employees—including upper management—concerning sexual harassment

- Implementing a grievance procedure where employees can resolve claims

- Informing all employees that the organization will discipline employees found guilty of sexual harassment, up to and including termination

What Actions Constitute Sexual Harassment? (from page 8)

1. **False.** Physical acts are only one form of sexual harassment. Jokes, comments, leers and cartoons with sexual undertones may also be considered sexual harassment.

2. **True.** The U.S. Supreme Court has said that acts that create a hostile or offensive work environment may constitute sexual harassment. A cartoon with sexual undertones may be considered sexual harassment if it creates a hostile or offensive environment.

3. **False.** Under most circumstances this will not be considered sexual harassment. It might, however, be considered discrimination on the basis of sex.

4. **True.** Actions by clients, customers or other nonemployees may constitute sexual harassment. The employer who knows of the actions and takes no steps to stop them may be found legally liable.

5. **False.** Sexual harassment is a very personal matter. If "unwelcome," staring or leering could be considered sexual harassment.

6. **False.** These are the type of actions that may create a hostile or offensive work environment.

7. **False.** Unpermitted or unwelcome acts are the essence of sexual harassment.

8. **False.** Acts of sexual harassment affect not only the direct participants, but others who may be denied employment opportunities or who work in the same area.

9. **True.** This is the *quid pro quo* situation.

10. **True.** This is true if the subordinate believes that rejection may result in adverse employment action.

ANSWERS AND SOLUTIONS (continued)

Why Training? (from page 44)

☐ The first situation is a classic example of harassment.

☐ The second question is more complex. If the women consider this behavior harassing, the organization should protect itself by dealing with it.

☐ The third situation is even more complex. It addresses the question of whether a woman is responsible for comments that anyone makes about her when she wears suggestive clothing. Certainly, if she considers the men's comments as sexually harassing, this is an incident of harassment. A workplace can head off this kind of problem by setting acceptable standards for dress. It is appropriate for her manager to discuss with her what is considered appropriate attire for work. This should have been done before the harassment occurred.

☐ In most workplaces, calendars of nudes are inappropriate. The manager should talk to the individual about this and see that he removes the calendar.

☐ This is another classic boss and subordinate case. The gender of the persons involved is irrelevant. If the man feels that his female boss is harassing him, she is. It would be appropriate for him to tell her he feels uncomfortable with the situation and feels it is inappropriate for a work relationship. Since she is his boss, he must approach this very carefully.

☐ The situation with the client is an example of circumstances in which an employer can be liable for the harassing behavior of a client. Since the individual is a major client, this is a very sensitive situation.

☐ The final situation is not a case of sexual harassment. Nevertheless, such a case would have to be investigated in much the same manner, comparing performances of the individuals involved.

Case Study—XYZ Corporation (from page 59)

This is a case of discrimination and harassment, but not sexual harassment. It demonstrates one of the advantages of having an overall policy that covers all forms of harassment (see pages 37 and 38), rather than one that only covers sexual harassment. Alex Jordan will need to talk to George Strong and tell him emphatically that his behavior is not acceptable and must cease. If the company has a strong policy, this will be easier since Alex can quote the company policy. Alex should first give a verbal warning and back it up with documentation in George Strong's file. If George does not stop, Alex will need to give him a written warning and explain that unless this behavior ceases, he may be terminated. Once again, a policy backed up by a procedure provides the company with a much stronger case.

Since the problem is apparently "spreading," Alex should meet with all his workers in appropriate groups to discuss the company's overall stance on harassment, as well as the legal issues involved. Before he does this Alex should consult human resources for guidance. Alex should document everything he does.

> **NOTE:** Discrimination against homosexuals is not prohibited by federal law or the EEOC guidelines. However, some states and cities do have such laws. Regardless, sexual harassment against homosexuals is not permitted.

ANSWERS AND SOLUTIONS (continued)

Counseling (from page 64)

The first thing to do is to provide Sally a safe place to talk and ventilate her feelings. She is probably angry, hurt and afraid. Discuss alternatives with Sally. One alternative would be to tell Sally how she can approach the vice president and explain to him that she does not believe in mixing work and social relationships. This may require considerable coaching and some role playing. Show Sally how she can remain polite while refusing his advances. She might say, for example, ''Mr. Smith, I am flattered by your asking me out. However, I have a strong belief against mixing social and work relationships. This has nothing to do with you personally. I trust you will understand. I love my job and feel I am making a real contribution here.''

She needs to be prepared for some anger. Ask her to report the results to you.

Of course, if the vice president has seen her go out with anyone else, she may have to change her tactics. The situation will be more difficult because she will not be able to use separation of social and work relationships in the same manner.

Note: This identical situation could easily occur if the gender of the individuals is reversed or if the persons are of the same gender.

Another alternative would be to handle the matter yourself, if you are the appropriate person in your organization; you could refer her to human resources if you are not. The complaint should be handled using the investigative procedures suggested in this book.

If Sally chooses to handle it herself first, she will need support and encouragement. If her attempts fail, the situation must be investigated.

NOTES

FOR OTHER FIFTY-MINUTE SELF-STUDY BOOKS
SEE THE BACK OF THIS BOOK.

NOTES

FOR OTHER FIFTY-MINUTE SELF-STUDY BOOKS
SEE THE BACK OF THIS BOOK.

ABOUT THE FIFTY-MINUTE SERIES

We hope you enjoyed this book and found it valuable. If so, we have good news for you. This title is part of the best selling *FIFTY-MINUTE Series* of books. All *Series* books are similar in size and format, and identical in price. Several are supported with training videos. These are identified by the symbol **v** next to the title.

Since the first *FIFTY-MINUTE* book appeared in 1986, millions of copies have been sold worldwide. Each book was developed with the reader in mind. The result is a concise, high quality module written in a positive, readable self-study format.

FIFTY-MINUTE Books and Videos are available from your distributor. A free current catalog is available on request from Crisp Publications, Inc., 95 First Street, Los Altos, CA 94022.

Following is a complete list of *FIFTY-MINUTE Series* Books and Videos organized by general subject area.